TH

MW01035149

NOTES

including
- *Life and Background*
- *General Introduction*
- *List of Characters*
- *Commentary*
- *Notes on Main Characters*
- *Critical Notes on the Code Hero,*
  Ideology, Style
- *Review Questions and Theme Topics*
- *Selected Bibliography*

by
LaRocque DuBose, M.A.
Dept. of Languages and Literature
Western State College of Colorado

INCORPORATED

LINCOLN, NEBRASKA 68501

Editor

Gary Carey, M.A.
University of Colorado

Consulting Editor

James L. Roberts, Ph.D.
Department of English
University of Nebraska

ISBN 0-8220-0497-6
© Copyright 1965
by
Cliffs Notes, Inc.
All Rights Reserved
Printed in U.S.A.

1996 Printing

Cliffs Notes, Inc.   Lincoln, Nebraska

CONTENTS

Life and Background

In his earlier years Hemingway relished the nickname "Champ," which exemplified his roistering, hard-fisted outdoor life of adventure. In his later years, he delighted in being called "Papa" and had the reputation of a worldwide celebrities' celebrity, almost a legendary character. He often helped to further the legend in lively ways. During World War II, when he was an American war correspondent, there was no doubt who had helped liberate the Ritz hotel in Paris. A guard was found posted at the entrance with a notice, "Papa took good hotel. Plenty stuff in the cellar."

Hemingway's colorful life began in quiet Oak Park, Illinois, a suburb of Chicago, where he was born July 21, 1899. His father was a physician, and Ernest was the second of six children born to Dr. and Mrs. Clarence E. Hemingway. His mother, a devout, religious woman with considerable musical talent, hoped that Ernest would develop an interest in music. Ernest acquired his father's enthusiasm for guns and for fishing trips in the Michigan north woods, and that phase of his childhood formed important impressions reflected later in Nick Adams stories like "Indian Camp" and "Big Two-Hearted River."

Hemingway played high school football and learned to box, incurring permanent eye damage that caused the army to reject his repeated efforts to enlist in World War I. Boxing also gave Hemingway a lasting enthusiasm for prize fighting, material for stories, and a tendency to talk of his literary accomplishments later in boxing terms.

He edited the high school newspaper, twice ran away from home, and on graduating from high school, Hemingway headed for Kansas City to enlist despite parental objections that he was too young—seventeen. Rejected by the army, he went to the Kansas City *Star,* a national newspaper, where he added a year to his age and was hired as a reporter. (For that reason Hemingway's birth date is often given as 1898 rather than the correct 1899.)

Finally, Hemingway succeeded in joining a volunteer American Red Cross ambulance unit as a driver. He was so seriously wounded at Fossalta on the Italian Piave on July 8, 1918, that he recalled life slid from him, "like you'd pull a silk handkerchief out of a pocket by a corner," almost fluttered away, then returned. It is thought by some literary observers that the experience gave Hemingway a fear of his own fear and the lifetime need to continually test his courage through dangerous adventures.

After a dozen operations on his knee and recuperation in Milan, he returned, with an aluminum kneecap and two Italian decorations, to join the Italian infantry. These vivid experiences later provided background for *A Farewell to Arms* in 1929.

War—the cruelty and stoic endurance that it requires—forms a major part of Hemingway's writing, beginning with the *In Our Time* collection published in 1924 to his post-World War II novel, *Across the River and Into the Trees*. In addition to World War I action, Hemingway later covered the Greek-Turkish War in 1920, while the Spanish Civil War in 1937 provided material for his *For Whom the Bell Tolls*.

Following World War I, Hemingway returned to northern Michigan to read, write, and fish, and then to work for the Toronto *Star* in Canada. He lived briefly in Chicago, where he came to know Sherwood Anderson. In 1921 he married Hadley Richardson and they moved to Paris, where he was foreign correspondent for the Toronto *Star*. His newsbeat was all of Europe, and while still in his twenties, Hemingway had interviewed Lloyd George, Clemenceau, and Mussolini. The years 1921-26 in Paris, when Hemingway was first developing his writing style and when his first son John was born, are recorded in *A Moveable Feast* (1964).

Sherwood Anderson had given Hemingway a letter of introduction to Gertrude Stein, who was living in Paris, and that proved to be his entrance into the world of working authors and artists who visited her home. It was she who mentioned a garage keeper's comment to Hemingway, "You are all a lost generation." That casual remark became famous when Hemingway used it as an epigraph to his first major novel, *The Sun Also Rises.*

"Lost generation" came to signify the postwar generation and the literary movement produced by the young writers. These writers of the twenties were thought to reflect that generation's belief that their lives and hopes had been shattered by the war. They had been led down a glory trail to death not for noble, patriotic ideals, but for the greedy, materialistic gain of power groups. The high-minded sentiments of their elders were not to be trusted. Only reality was truth and that was harsh. Life was futile — nothing.

F. Scott Fitzgerald, Sherwood Anderson, James Joyce, Ezra Pound, and Gertrude Stein are among those usually credited with influencing Hemingway's early writing. Most of that early work was lost when a suitcase containing the first draft of his first novel and eighteen of his stories representing most of four years work was stolen from his wife Hadley on a train to Lausanne, Switzerland. Later, "My Old Man," one of two short stories that Hemingway had left was selected for Edward O'Brien's volume of *Best Short Stories of 1923,* which was dedicated to Hemingway.

Early Hemingway stories had appeared in German and French publications before the *Atlantic Monthly* magazine published "Fifty Grand," the short story that introduced his startling concept of crisp, concise dialog to the United States. In 1923, *Three Stories and Ten Poems* was published, followed in 1924 by the Paris edition of *in our time.* (The lack of capital letters was the current vogue to call attention to newness.) In 1925 *In Our Time* was published in the United States by Boni and Liveright, Sherwood Anderson's publishers, who rejected Hemingway's next book, *The Torrents of Spring,* a satire of Anderson's *Dark Laughter.* Scribner's published the rejected manuscript and that same year issued Hemingway's first successful novel, *The Sun Also Rises* (1926).

The Hemingways were divorced in 1927, the same year that he married *Vogue* writer Pauline Pfeiffer. In 1928 the Hemingways moved to Key West, Florida, where Patrick was born in 1929 and Gregory in 1932. The shocking event of 1928 for Hemingway was the suicide of his father, who had been ill with hypertension and diabetes. It wasn't until 1940 that the experience was reflected in his writing through the thoughts of Robert Jordan in *For Whom the Bell Tolls,* and later characters sometimes expressed thoughts on suicide.

Between wars and books Hemingway traveled and pursued hunting and other sports. Bullfighting claimed his attention and resulted in *Death in the Afternoon.* His 1934 African safari yielded material for *The Snows of Kilimanjaro* and *Green Hills of Africa.*

In 1940, Hemingway and Pauline were divorced. He married writer Martha Gelhorn and they toured China before establishing in Cuba. When World War II began Hemingway volunteered his fishing boat, *Pilar,* and served with the U.S. Navy as a submarine spotter in the Caribbean. In 1944, he was a forty-five-year-old war correspondent barnstorming through Europe with the Allied invasion troops—and sometimes ahead of them.

Following his divorce in 1944, Hemingway married Mary Welsh, a *Time* magazine correspondent. They lived in Venice after the war before returning to *Finca Vigia* (Lookout Farm) near Havana, Cuba. In 1950, *Across the River and Into the Trees* appeared and was not a critical success. One of the reported comments was, "Papa is finished." His 1952 work, *The Old Man and the Sea* received the 1953 Pulitzer Prize.

In January of 1954 Hemingway was off for another African hunt and was reported dead after two airplane crashes in two days. He survived severe internal and spinal injuries and a concussion that impaired his eyesight for a period. He survived to read the numerous newspaper obituary notices and noted with great pleasure that they were favorable. That same year Hemingway received the Swedish Academy's Nobel Prize for Literature, "for his powerful style-forming mastery of the art of modern narration, as most recently evinced in *The Old Man and the Sea.*

Suddenly he was sixty and there was his birthday photograph in a national magazine. White-bearded and still full of ginger, Hemingway was booting an empty beer can high in the air along a road near his Ketchum, Idaho, home.

During 1961, Hemingway, plagued by high blood pressure and mental depression, received shock treatments during two long confinements at the Mayo Clinic in Rochester, Minnesota. He died July 2, 1961, at his home in Ketchum, Idaho, as the result of self-inflicted gunshot wounds and was buried in Ketchum.

In a manner, there were two Hemingways. One was the flamboyant adventurer—the lively legend in the spotlight. The other Hemingway was the skillful, sensitive author who patiently wrote, rewrote, and edited his work. *A Farewell to Arms* (1929) required eight months for writing the first draft and another five months for rewriting, according to Hemingway, who claimed to have rewritten the last page thirty-nine times. That writing discipline begun in the twenties persisted throughout his literary career. In discussing *The Old Man and the Sea* (1952), Hemingway is said to have read through the manuscript some two hundred times before releasing it. Hemingway, the colorful legend, was also the author who said, "What many another writer would be content to leave in massive proportions, I polish into a tiny gem."

General Introduction

For Whom the Bell Tolls, published in 1940, grew out of Hemingway's personal interest in the Spanish Civil War of the thirties. While still a foreign correspondent in Paris, Hemingway had watched the Spanish political situation developing under the reign of Alfonso XIII. He had visited Spain again during the summer of 1931 after the overthrow of the monarchy. He predicted the civil war would begin in 1935 and when it erupted in 1936, Hemingway began writing and making speeches to raise funds for the Loyalist cause. Later in 1937, he went to Spain to cover the war for the North American Newspaper Alliance. In reality, the Spanish Civil War was the first battleground for World War II, testing the forces of Nazism, Communism, and Fascism against either the republican or royal form of government. Many young men from the United States and other countries joined the Spanish Loyalist forces in defense of democratic ideals in a war that was won by the dictator, Francisco Franco. Since that war has tended to slip into the dimness of the shadow cast by World War II, the following review of historical and biographical background should clarify a number of things pertinent to the novel.

In the spring of 1931, after several years of civil strife and strikes, municipal elections were held in Spain. The parliamentary seats won in this election were divided between the leftists and rightists in such a way that an extremely dangerous situation was created. In view of this, and in the hope of avoiding civil war, King Alfonso XIII decided on voluntary exile. On April 13, 1931, the republic was proclaimed.

The Communist-Socialist coalition which ruled Spain during the first two years of the republic was, like its predecessors, plagued by strikes, and a general election was called for November, 1933. In this election, the rightists were returned to power with a large majority.

The Conservatives were, however, only able to keep themselves in power for about the same length of time that the leftists had. By February, 1936, when another general election was held, public opinion had swung back to its previous position. The leftists won this election by a small majority — 256 seats to 217 for the Conservatives.

Five months after the leftists regained control of the government, José Calvas Otelo, a powerful Monarchist-rightist, was assassinated. This was credited with precipitating a revolt which was led by the army, but which had obviously been planned for some time. General Francisco Franco was recalled from the Canary Islands, where he had been sent to keep him out of politics. He flew to Spanish Morocco on July 17 and quickly overthrew the government there, continuing on to Spain the next day.

Within a few hours after Franco's arrival in Spain, his forces had taken several of the larger Spanish cities, and garrisons of the army all over Spain were in revolt. Surprising and stubborn resistance from the government's militia brought this initial surge to a temporary halt, and the capital city of Madrid remained in the hands of the Loyalist-leftists.

Foreign intervention in this revolt which had turned into a civil war was an accomplished fact by August of 1936. Russia was sending "observers" and volunteers" as well as financial aid donated by its citizens to help in the leftist cause, but they were not industrially capable of giving a great deal of aid in the form of material. In support of the Monarchist-rightists, both Germany and Italy sent planes, tanks, and munitions in addition to the usual "observers" and "volunteers."

The quickly formed Loyalist-leftist forces managed to bring the war to a stalemate during the winter of 1936-37, but this situation was only temporary. By the spring of 1937 (the time during which the incidents of *For Whom the Bell Tolls* occur), the leftists had, however, gathered enough men and equipment to prevent Franco from overrunning the country. The Monarchist offensive proceeded, but slowly.

International politics played a great part in the civil war during the next two years, giving the advantage first to one side and then to the other. Throughout this period both sides committed sickening atrocities. The Loyalists were charged with the murders of hundreds of members of the clergy as well as the assassination of their political enemies, and the systematic bombing and strafing of nonmilitary objectives by the Monarchists was a portent of things to come in World War II.

By January of 1939, an almost completely effective blockade was preventing Loyalist troops from receiving further munitions and supplies. Resistance in towns and cities which had managed so far to hold out against Franco's troops began to collapse. Finally, on March 28, 1939, the well supplied Monarchist forces overcame the resistance of the besieged city of Madrid. The long and bitter civil war was over.

After World War I, Hemingway returned to the United States, but, by 1921 he was married and back in Europe as a foreign correspondent. He traveled extensively in Spain and was vitally interested in the political developments during the reign of Alfonso XIII, from 1923 until 1931. In 1928 he moved to Key West, Florida, and so was not present for the overthrow of the monarchy in 1931. He returned to Spain for a visit that summer, however, and learned what had happened from his friends there.

When the Conservatives were returned to power in 1933, Hemingway was traveling in Africa. He was not surprised by the failure of the liberal government for two reasons. First, he felt that "the mass of the people were not ready for it and did not want it." Second, though Spain had become more prosperous under the liberals, and though he agreed at least in principle with the civil reforms instituted by them, he realized that the peasants were receiving very little benefit from the government. The money was going where it had always gone—into the pockets of those in power.

Between 1933 and 1936, Hemingway carefully watched the political developments in Spain. When the civil war finally began in 1936, the only surprising thing to him was that it had come so soon, for as early as the summer of 1935 he had predicted that war would come before the end of the decade.

In 1936 and 1937, Hemingway wrote and made speeches for the purpose of raising money for the Loyalist cause in the Spanish Civil War. Later in 1937, he went to Spain to cover the war for the North American Newspaper Alliance. His announcement, some months after he arrived in Spain, that he was writing a novel with the Spanish Civil War as its background, caused a great stir of excitement and anticipation in the literary world. The result was *For Whom the Bell Tolls.*

List of Characters

Robert Jordan
An American college instructor of Spanish, fighting as a demolition expert with the Loyalists in the Spanish Civil War.

Pablo
Leader of the guerilla band whose aid Jordan enlists in the destruction of a bridge.

Pilar
Pablo's *mujer,* who has kept the band together in spite of the fact that Pablo has "gone bad."

Maria
A young girl whom the guerillas have rescued from enemy captivity and who falls in love with Jordan.

Anselmo
An old man, one of the few members of Pablo's band whom Jordan trusts.

General Golz
A Russian officer, one of the many military "observers" sent to aid the Spanish communists in the war, who is directing the forthcoming attack.

Kashkin
Another Russian, Jordan's predecessor as demolition man with Pablo's band. He is dead when the book opens.

El Sordo
The leader of another guerilla band which is hiding out in the vicinity of Pablo's cave.

Joaquin
A young boy, member of El Sordo's band.

Eladio
Agustin
Andres
Fernando   Members of Pablo's band.
Primitivo
Rafael

Gypsy

Commentary

CHAPTERS 1-7

Hemingway develops several themes in the course of *For Whom the Bell Tolls*. Before we examine the themes which make their appearance in this section, certain facts about the bitterly fought Spanish Civil War should be explained. First, that the war was a completely undisguised war between communism and fascism. Within a month after its beginning, Russia on the one hand and Germany and Italy on the other were using it as a training and testing ground for their men, techniques, and equipment. Second, though in recent years communism has adopted a "soft" policy toward religion, in the communism of the Spanish Civil War religion was completely done away with.

The first theme which makes its appearance in the book is what might be called the theme of "mysticism-superstition." Robert Jordan thinks that it is a "bad sign" that he has forgotten Anselmo's name. This idea of "signs" and "luck" is simply introduced in this chapter, but it is developed to a much greater degree as the book moves on. Its importance in the psychological makeup of Robert Jordan will become more apparent in later chapters.

One of the major ideas in a large part of Hemingway's writing is the irony of life. In Chapter 1, it is tied in with the cynicism of the people involved in the war. We see it first in the scene between Jordan and Golz in which they discuss the proposed attack. The Russian general is interested in the offensive mainly as a military maneuver, and he is cynical because he knows that the Spanish will interfere.

The irony becomes obvious when this same cynicism is expressed by Pablo. The guerilla leader resents the fact that a foreigner has come to tell him what to do. This puts Pablo into a subservient position where he is no longer the spokesman or leader of the group. Consequently, one of the major conflicts in the novel involves Pablo's qualifications as a leader. From his point of view, he is interested only in the preservation of his band and himself. The military maneuvers of foreigners is of little importance to him. Also, Pablo has recently become the owner of a number of fine horses, making him a capitalist for the first time in his life. As a result, he is not nearly so interested in fighting for the cause as he once was, and this adds further to the ironic theme.

This theme of irony, of the relationship between the individuals — the "little people," for whose benefit wars are, ostensibly, fought — and the politico-military machine, is interwoven with other themes throughout the book, but it is the major theme of *For Whom the Bell Tolls*.

The first chapter, as might be expected, is largely introductory. It is to Hemingway's credit as an artist, however, that it is not blatantly so. This subtlety is accomplished primarily by virtue of the fact that he allows the reader to *deduce* the situation. For instance, within 500 words after the opening of the book Robert Jordan has, through his dialog, told the reader that he is carrying explosives and that he is most interested in the bridge. Thus we already know, by the time we are told so specifically some 1,000 words later, that Jordan's mission is to destroy the bridge.

This same subtlety is apparent in Hemingway's introduction of his characters. In fact, rather than to say that he *introduces* his characters, I would prefer to use a term from the drama and say that they *make their entrance*. Three of the most important characters do appear in this first chapter — the protagonist, Robert Jordan, his guide, Anselmo, and the guerilla leader, Pablo. Though we are given physical descriptions of these three men which range from merely adequate, as in the case of Anselmo, to vivid, as in the case of Pablo, most important is the fact that we are made acutely aware of their characters.

And so the stage is set. We know, almost from the beginning, that the main dramatic situation is the problem of destroying the bridge. We know, from the flashback scene between Jordan and

General Golz, that the manner in which the mission is to be accomplished is highly unorthodox and, therefore, highly dangerous. And we know that there is a dangerous conflict of personalities between Jordan and Pablo.

The main action in Chapter 3 is that Jordan and Anselmo go to look at the bridge, but it is a very important chapter, because the moral problems of war are introduced in the conversation between Jordan and Anselmo. Jordan has considered himself an instrument of a war which is being fought for the good of the common people. Thus, while he was idealistic about the aims of the war, he had forced himself to ignore the damage war does to the individual.

So far, Robert Jordan has been pictured as being what any good fighter for a cause should be. He is developing into the Hemingway "code" hero. (See the section entitled "The Hemingway Code Hero.") He is skilled in his work, he is dedicated, he is determined to carry out his orders, since he knows that they are always for the good of the Cause, and he is willing to sacrifice himself as well as others for the Cause. In this chapter, however, we see the suggestion of a change coming over his character. When he sees how simple it would have been to destroy the bridge in the normal way, he resents the fact that he must do it in an unorthodox, dangerous way. He begins to have the first glimmerings of the idea that perhaps a cause is not always worth the lives of the individuals who die for it, but he brushes the idea aside, not wanting to think such thoughts.

Another underlying purpose of Chapter 3 is the characterization of the simple peasants who make up Pablo's band of guerillas. It is shown best in the scene of comic relief in which Jordan and Anselmo are stopped by the guard who has forgotten the password. Agustin is tired, hungry, uncomfortable, and bored, he would rather be almost any place than to be engaged in a war.

The ominous note on which the previous chapter ends, reverberates with increasing volume in Chapter 4.

Pablo's announcement that he is against blowing up the bridge creates a crisis. When Pilar says that she is for destroying the bridge, the men side with her, not because they feel that it is their duty, but because Pablo has "gone bad" — another demonstration of the lack of interest of the individual in dying for a cause. The attitude of the men toward the bridge is obviously one of indifference. In fact, they would really rather blow up another train. There was looting at the train which they destroyed earlier, and they had taken a childish delight in the explosion and ensuing wreck. They would like to relive this moment of glory, the high point of their war career. Pablo tries to use this feeling in his argument against the bridge, assuming that the men are most interested in gaining material wealth, such as his own herd of horses.

The near-showdown in Chapter 4 has left Jordan with a problem. Should he have killed Pablo? As much as he dislikes the idea of assassination, he feels that he probably should have, especially when the gypsy tells him that the entire band was waiting for him to kill Pablo. Jordan loses the initiative in the situation when Pablo joins him outside the cave and tries to be friendly. To kill the guerilla leader now would simply be cold-blooded murder.

In Chapter 3, we first saw signs of a subtle change in Jordan's attitude toward this war. That change becomes evident again here. In former days, he would not have hesitated a moment before killing Pablo, but now he gives himself a whole series of excuses for not having done so. He feels that he should take no useless risks, and he maintains that it was not clear to him that the gypsies expected him to kill Pablo. Mainly, he excuses himself by saying that he did not know how Pilar would have reacted to the slaying. When Pablo goes to see about the horses, Jordan hopes that one of the others will kill him, but he knows they will not.

As for poor Pablo, he is homesick and he is tired of the war and he does not want to be killed, either by his own people or in the battle of the bridge. He strokes his horse and talks to it gently, but even the horse is relieved when he finally moves the picket pin and stops bothering him.

The nature of the philosophy behind the Republican movement is revealed here in both positive and negative terms. Jordan objects to being called "Don Roberto," because only the ruling class were addressed as "Don" under the previous form of government. That the people for whom the war is supposedly being fought do not take the matter so seriously, is a part of Hemingway's theme of ironic contrasts.

The scene of wry humor in which Jordan makes the most of the double meaning of "republican" leads Maria into a feeling of rapport with the American and makes her embryonic love for him begin to grow. The question of Pablo returns, also. Jordan brings up the matter of whether or not he should have killed him, but Pilar says that he was right in not doing so. She, unlike Jordan, understands the change that has begun to come over the guerilla leader.

In spite of all attempts to remain aloof from emotional involvements and to maintain a coldly critical attitude toward his work, Jordan finally finds himself falling in love. There is some contrast between his emotions and his surroundings, but the main item here is the contrast between Maria's rape at the hands of her fascist captors and the act of love between her and Jordan.

CHAPTERS 8-13

The appearance of the unusually large number of enemy aircraft at the beginning of Chapter 8 serves two purposes. The fact that there are many enemy planes in the area indicates that the fascists either know about the planned communist offensive or are planning an attack of their own in the sector. The large number of planes serves, by contrast, to point out the fact that the fascists are being much better supplied with weapons than are the communists.

Whether the planes mean a fascist offensive is coming, or that the fascists know a communist offensive is coming, the situation has become critical. Fernando's arrival with rumors of a Loyalist attack is further proof that the fascists are expecting that attack. Jordan is appalled at this inexcusable leak in security.

Jordan's thoughts about the lackadaisical way in which the Spaniards are running their war (and here we must remember that it is not really the Spaniards who *are* running it) are interrupted by Pilar's reminiscing about the "good old days" in Valencia. One gets the feeling in this scene that these people would almost prefer a more "usual" kind of existence, even under the fascists, to fighting in this war for their own liberation.

Several themes which have already made their appearance are brought back into view in Chapter 9. The fact that the enemy is better equipped is re-emphasized by Jordan's explanation that their side does not have enough planes to start an offensive. The religious theme is also reintroduced, though it is just barely touched upon as Pilar says that God still exists even though they have tried to abolish Him.

Jordan's battle within himself has now passed the beginning stage. He speaks to Pilar of "duty," but he acknowledges that he cares very much for Maria, and he is still worried about what it was that Pilar saw when she read his palm.

Pablo's sudden deterioration is mentioned again, but we find that he may regain a great deal of his importance after all, since he is the best equipped to get them away safely after the bridge has been blown.

Here, too, as in previous chapters and in the chapters to come, there is much lip service paid to the idea that "we must win." But it is hardly more than lip service. It is obvious that the enemy is better equipped. It is obvious that they cannot be defeated. It is obvious that the war is "an idiocy without bounds." And it is becoming less and less obvious to all of them that it is worth their lives and the lives of others like them.

Chapter 10 serves one major purpose in the book, and that is to demonstrate that the "good guys" display just as much cruelty in a war as do the "bad guys." In masterly fashion, Hemingway shows also, in this chapter, that both sides are made up of individual human beings with their individual hopes, fears, and desires. Among the Loyalists in Pilar's story are those who do not like what is going on and do not want any of the captives killed, but many of these are afraid not to participate for fear of being brought under suspicion themselves. There are those who succumb to the mob hysteria and become raving beasts out for blood, and there are those, like Pablo, who enjoy the massacre immensely. Among the Monarchists in Pilar's story are those who cringe before their captors and plead for mercy. There are those who, in a horror-induced catatonic state, do not seem to understand what has happened or why they are being so treated. And there are those who face their captors scornfully, and defiantly shout insults at their executioners.

Nearly every possible human reaction to the situation described by Pilar is artfully brought out here by Hemingway. How better could he emphasize the fact that, whether Monarchist or Loyalist, it is those whom the Spanish themselves would call *la gente* (the people) who are involved in the struggle?

Chapter 11 is devoted to filling in some of the blank spaces left in earlier chapters. The reader learns more of the details of the rescue of Maria. He learns, too, the details of Kashkin's death. He also gets further information about the danger connected with blowing up the bridge. The reader, however, is not left for long to feel sorry for the poor fascists whose murders Pilar described in the previous chapter. Jordan's thoughts, upon hearing of the death of Joaquin's family, serve to enlighten the reader as to the cruel practices of the Monarchists.

The Kashkin theme, which, by comparing Jordan with his predecessor, carries a tone of premonition, makes another appearance here. In fact, Pilar brings Kashkin into the conversation because of this tone. She feels that Jordan has bragged too much about what he and his kind have done in the war, so she "takes him down a peg" by reminding him of the similarity between himself and Kashkin.

Chapter 12, by dramatizing Pilar's mood, "sets the reader up" for Jordan's thoughts in the first part of the next chapter.

The discussion with El Sordo has made Pilar realize the real seriousness and danger of the bridge operation; this is the reason for her sudden ill temper. Jordan knows that Pablo's sullenness upon hearing of the bridge operation was based on his immediate understanding of the danger involved. He also has seen that El Sordo, too, grasped the real nature of the problem very quickly. And now, he realizes, Pilar has come to understand.

The love theme, played mostly in little *pianissimo* snatches in earlier chapters, swells to a crescendo in Chapter 13. Jordan wants to live. He wants to live out a normal life with Maria as his wife. He does not want to die for a Cause. What are they fighting against, anyway? They are fighting against just exactly those things which they are doing themselves—things they were forced to do if they were to stand any chance of winning.

Jordan argues bitterly with himself. It is true that they are doing many of the things which they condemned in their enemies, but in this case the enemies were the leaders of Spain. Then he realizes that the phrase "enemies of the people" is one of the stock phrases of the communists. He has associated with the communists so closely and for so long that he has started using the clichés easily and uncritically. This disgusts him, for now he has no politics. His love for Maria (and he admits to himself now that, for the first time, he is truly in love) has made him see the situation clearly.

Besides revealing further details of Jordan's personal background, his lengthy consideration of his position brings out one of the two instances of irony in the chapter. When has he met the person whom he can truly love? Seventy-two hours before he must blow up a bridge in an unnecessarily dangerous manner and, probably, die. The other instance of irony comes at the end of the chapter when it becomes obvious that, even though it is May, it is going to snow. Not only must the guerillas retreat in daylight, but their tracks will be easily followed.

CHAPTERS 14-21

Though the main part of Chapter 14 is taken up by Pilar's story of the bullfighter, her tale is sandwiched between two important scenes. Pablo assumes that the blowing up of the bridge will be called off, and he tells Jordan that he need not go for the scouts because they will come in out of the snow even though they were ordered to wait for Jordan to come to them. Jordan curses his bad luck, but indicates that the job will proceed as planned, anyhow. He is inclined to believe that Pablo is right about the scouts; the whole war is being fought in just such a lackadaisical way, after all. The second scene comes at the end of the chapter when the gypsy does, indeed, leave his post and return to the cave. Nor, since he is cold and hungry, will he go with Jordan to show him where Anselmo is.

Pilar's story is itself important because it gives additional background material about life before the movement. Bullfighting is one of the few ways in which a man could raise himself above his station. Pilar's friend paid a dreadful price, however. Though almost dying of consumption, he feels that he must stay in the tavern to satisfy his fans. But when, at the climax of the evening, they unveil the mounted bull's head, the bullfighter is horror-stricken. His courage, drained away by his illness and injuries, has finally left him.

In Chapter 15, the reader finds Anselmo who, uncharacteristically for most of the guerillas and soldiers, has stayed at his post waiting for Jordan. He thinks of all the people whose lives are disrupted or ended by the war. He does not want to kill. All day he has been watching the fascist guards and he feels a close identification with them. He feels that he could walk over to the mill where the guards are and that they would welcome him, except that they have orders to challenge all travelers. "It is only orders that come between us," he thinks. "Those men are not fascists. . . . They are poor men as we are." Then Hemingway takes the reader across the road and into the mill to witness the conversation between the fascist soldiers. Indeed, they are just the kind of people that Anselmo has thought they were.

While Chapters 16 and 17 serve mainly to bring the serious problem of Pablo to a temporary head, they also furnish the reader additional information which he has not previously had. Primitivo's questions about America, for instance, demonstrate the nature of some of Spain's political problems. Jordan's answers, in turn, show his feeling that the fascistic ills of the world will someday have to be corrected.

The fact is also brought out that Jordan was an instructor of Spanish in America. And Fernando, who symbolizes the formality and prudishness of the lower-middle-class Spaniard of that time, provides comic relief to the scene when he complains at length that a foreigner should not be allowed to teach Spanish.

In Chapter 17, the decision to kill Pablo is made and abandoned when Pablo returns in a friendly and cooperative mood. Pilar indicates to Jordan that Pablo's change of heart has undoubtedly come about because he overheard the plans to kill him. But when Pablo points out that he is the only one who can lead them to safety after the bridge, the assassination is tacitly canceled. However, Pablo still remains a real threat to the success of the operation.

The student will probably have noticed by now that Hemingway seldom allows one of his scenes to have only a single purpose. This multiplicity of purpose is evident in Chapter 18, the basic ingredient of which is Jordan's thoughts about Gaylord's. The flashback reveals Jordan's disillusionment at finding so much cynicism in the meeting place of the communists. He discovers that the emotional appeal of the Cause is ridiculed by those whose job it is to make the appeal. He learns that the leaders of the movement, who were supposed to have been peasants who rose to command at the hour of need, were really members of an earlier revolution who had fled Spain and been trained in Russia for the next revolution. And he discovers that those who naively believe in the humanitarian doctrines of communism are laughed at, but that they are catered to so long as they are useful.

In the beginning, Jordan hates the lying and cynicism, but he comes to realize the necessity for it. He feels that he has progressed through the three Hegelian steps from "thesis" to "antithesis" to "synthesis," but this is not true. He is not fully aware, at this point in the book, that he is still what Pablo has called him a short time earlier, one of the "illusioned ones."

In addition to the main idea of this chapter, Hemingway gives the reader additional bits of information, some of which has been given before and is here simply being re-emphasized. We find, for instance, that Jordan is enough of a writer to have had a book published. We are told again that he was a college teacher, and that he may not be able to teach again because of his political sympathies. And, in the scene involving the armored car, we see again the unwillingness of the peasants to die for the Cause.

The primary purpose of Chapter 19 is, of course, obvious. The problem of Pablo has been temporarily resolved, and Hemingway does not want his reader to become too contented, so he reintroduces the theme of mysticism, which bears along with it the premonition of tragedy.

The theme of mysticism is one of the most fascinating of the minor (but important) themes which run through *For Whom the Bell Tolls*. It is first encountered on the second page of the text when Jordan feels that it is a "bad sign" that he has forgotten Anselmo's name. And it reappears again and again throughout the book, first as part of the "Kashkin theme" and again in relation to what Pilar has seen in Jordan's palm. In Chapter 19, the idea is brought out overtly by Hemingway and discussed openly by his characters.

The highly superstitious nature of gypsies is well known, of course, so the supernatural beliefs of Pilar and Rafael are understandable. But what of the others? None of the rest of the band, except Pablo, dismisses the idea of mysticism as summarily as does Jordan. Hemingway seems here to be emphasizing again the proneness of these people to mystical belief, especially at a time when the mysticism of their church has been denied them by the revolution.

The conversation in Chapter 19 has had its effect on Jordan. His momentary detour into homesickness and the urgency of his desire for Maria show that he is afraid that they have little time left. The fear is shown again when Jordan awakes in the night and holds her tightly, as though he were afraid of losing her.

Chapter 21 is devoted primarily to physical action; Jordan's fears seem to be turning into reality. But he is now the soldier, no longer the lover, as he dispatches the men and weapons strategically. Nevertheless, Hemingway takes another opportunity to bring in the mystical-religious theme again. He does this by having Maria ask about the medal worn by the cavalryman whom Jordan has just shot. Then Jordan has to take the time to assure her that he had not aimed at the Sacred Heart badge worn by the soldier.

CHAPTERS 22-32

Here begins the slow build-up of emotional tension which will have as its climax the battle at the bridge. Since the physical action over the next few chapters is restricted — the guerillas are simply manning their posts, waiting to see if anything happens — Hemingway takes the opportunity to refresh the reader's memory on several points.

First, he lets the reader see again how sloppily the war is being handled. Rafael deserts his post to chase a couple of rabbits, thereby letting the cavalryman slip through. Jordan finds that the machine gun has been sent to them with no instructions as to how to fire it or place it properly.

Later, the problem of Pablo is brought up again. Agustin tries to convince Jordan that Pablo is still a very smart guerilla leader. Jordan is already aware of this, but his personal dislike for Pablo has made him deny the man the credit he deserves for having successfully evaded capture for so long.

Then, Hemingway re-establishes the character of Anselmo. When Agustin says that they (the Loyalists) will have to kill many people after they have won the war, Anselmo disagrees. His conscience bothers him terribly about the killing he has done and will have to do. All he wants to do is win the war and then to govern justly and educate those who have fought against them so that they will see their error.

In Chapters 24 through 26, the tension continues to build, now based on the theme of irony. Agustin has told Jordan that El Sordo's band is much better than Pablo's but, almost immediately, they realize that El Sordo has been attacked and surrounded by the cavalry. The irony is continued in Jordan's thoughts about the soldier whom he has killed. Though he has thought, in the previous chapter, that he has grown to like the killing, he now admits to himself that of the twenty men he has killed only two of them were really fascists.

The reader also finds Jordan once again engaged in a struggle with his conscience. He questions again his political beliefs, acknowledging the fact that he has never believed in the purely materialistic conception of society held by the communists. He tells himself that he believes in "Liberty, Equality and Fraternity," and in "Life, Liberty and the Pursuit of Happiness." Though neither communism or fascism offers these things, the main problem is to get rid of the present enemies of the people. Later, one can decide what not to believe in.

Chapter 27 involves the young and innocent Joaquin. He has been taught the stock communist phrases of La Pasionaria, he has believed them, and now he bravely tries to keep up the spirits of his comrades by repeating them. He refuses to believe that the peasant generals have been trained in Russia and that others like himself have been sent to the safety of Russia to study. But he adds, in his naively conventional concern for the Cause, that he hopes they study well and come back to help the people. At the end, though, he stops quoting the communist slogans and starts saying Hail Marys.

Hemingway has here another opportunity to show that the unwillingness to die for a Cause is not confined to the Loyalists. He does so by having the fascist captain unable to convince his men that the guerillas are dead and that they should go and investigate. The same scene indicates that the Loyalists are not alone in the idiotic manner in which they are running the war.

Irony, too, is present in this chapter. First, there is Joaquin's relapse into religion. Then there is El Sordo and his men, dying on the top of a useless "chancre of a hill." Finally, there is the irony that neither Lieutenant Berrendo and his men nor the guerillas really want to fight or die.

Hemingway, with characteristic irony, continues the religious theme which has been reintroduced in the previous chapter. As Lieutenant Berrendo rides down the hill in one direction, he is praying for the souls of the dead; as Anselmo walks down the hill in another direction, he too is praying—for the first time since the beginning of the movement.

Jordan's desire to remain alive continues to grow. Aware of this, he tries very hard to be sure that his message to Golz does not sound as if he wants the attack called off for personal reasons. He has little hope, though, that the offensive will be canceled. It is quite possible that the attack is not meant to succeed; it may be simply a holding action, or a diversionary movement to draw enemy troops away from another front. If this is the case, then the fact that the fascists are prepared for the attack will not make any difference to Golz.

In Chapter 30, Jordan's thoughts bring forth additional information for the reader. The courageous character of his grandfather is revealed, and we learn that his father had committed suicide—a shameful act of cowardice in Jordan's mind. Hemingway has shown in others of his works besides *For Whom the Bell Tolls* that his attitude toward suicide was the same as that of Robert Jordan. It was an ironic fate, indeed, that caused Hemingway, presumably, to take his own life.

In Chapter 31, though we have already been told that Maria is a "nice girl," we are now given additional specific details of her background. Her father was the mayor of the town, and her mother, though not a Republican, was loyal to her husband. Both died bravely, killed by a Falangist firing squad.

But the revelation of Maria's background is not the primary purpose of this chapter. Now, the intensity of a person's hopes and daydreams increases in proportion to the seriousness of his situation. The problem of the bridge has grown more and more hopeless up to this point, and Jordan's dream of taking Maria to Madrid is indicative of how little expectation he has of surviving the coming battle. Maria willingly joins Jordan in his dream, but there is desire on her part to "get everything said before it is too late." Jordan is also aware, from what Maria has said, that even Pilar has sought refuge in reverie during the day.

Chapter 32, though very brief, is overflowing with significance — not that this quality is unusual in Hemingway's writing. And most of this significance is intensified by the contrast between it and the chapters immediately preceding. At the same time that Jordan and Maria are wishfully making plans for a future which they do not really believe they will live to see, other Loyalists are having a gay, sophisticated party in Madrid. This ironic juxtaposition of events is one of Hemingway's favorite tricks. In fact, he specifically mentions this type of irony in one of his short stories by referring to the lines from W. H. Auden's poem, "Musee des Beaux Arts," which read, "... even the dreadful martyrdom must run its course/ Anyhow in a corner, some untidy spot/ Where the dogs go on with their doggy life and the torturer's horse/ Scratches its innocent behind on a tree."

The fact that the party is being held at all, much less in the besieged capital city, indicates the lack of concern for the war effort on the part of the foreign interventionists. The military leaders are irritated to learn that the coming offensive is no longer a secret — another reflection on the haphazard way the war is being run — but they are not surprised and they do nothing about the leakage of information.

The irony is continued when the rumor that the fascists are fighting among themselves is circulated. The fighting referred to is, of course, the battle in which El Sordo's band was wiped out. The final touch, though the reader cannot fully appreciate the irony at this point, comes when the general says that they can expect a message from Jordan during the night. Jordan has, indeed, sent a message, but the irony is not complete until the reader has discovered the fate of that message.

CHAPTERS 33-42

From this point to the end of the book, Hemingway develops two stories at the same time. Chapter 33 and subsequent alternate chapters carry the story of Jordan (except that Chapters 37-39 are all focused on Jordan). Chapter 34 and its succeeding alternate ones (with the exception mentioned above) carry the story of Andres, who is trying to get Jordan's message through to Golz. This plot device is the same one of "proximity" which Hemingway has used in Chapters 31 and 32. Here, however, he is not using the juxtaposition simply for its ironic effect, but has added the quality of suspense.

Jordan awakes, still in his hopeful frame of mind, thinking that it is Maria's hand which is shaking him. But he returns to reality rapidly when he learns that Pablo has vanished. The trusted Pilar has failed him. Jordan rebukes her, but then comforts her by assuring her that he can find another way to set off the explosion.

In Chapter 34, we discover that Andres is aware of what it is that he is fighting for. But he is relieved that he has been given the message to carry and will probably not get back in time for the fighting. He compares his relief to that which he had felt in his boyhood when he had awakened on *fiesta* day to find that it was raining and that the bull-baiting would be canceled. Not that he was not brave at the bull-baiting. In fact, he had been nicknamed "Bulldog" because he always grabbed the bull's ear and bit it during the final rush on the bull.

Andres does not lack courage, but he is here exemplifying one of the major ideas which has been brought out again and again in the book. He does not wish to die for the Cause. He does not really care much about fighting for it. He realizes that his enemies are simply other men like himself and that they are his enemies only because of a trick of fate. He reminisces about the happy days with his brother during their youth, and he wishes he could return to them. Then he knows that he must try to get back in time to help his brother and the others.

In Chapter 35, Jordan is furious with himself for having for-gotten what he had known back in the first chapter—that Pablo would only be friendly in order to betray him.

And he is furious with Spain and with every Spaniard on either side. They are selfish, egotistical, treacherous, cowardly, undisci-plined. But as his rage becomes more and more exaggerated, he realizes that he is being unjust. He decides that the situation is not as bad as he had thought. They will be killed, but they will blow the bridge.

The final sentence of the chapter is another excellent example of Hemingway's use of irony. Jordan lies by the sleeping Maria, holding her lightly and feeling the life in her, but at the same time he is keeping track of the time on his wrist watch.

After reading Chapter 36, one might tend to think that Jordan had been somewhat hasty in the preceding chapter in deciding that his criticism of the Spaniards was unjust. The comic relief of the chapter is accomplished with typical Hemingway humor—there is a serious and very unfunny basis underlying it. While Andres is trying desperately to get Jordan's message to Golz in time for the attack to be canceled, the soldiers on guard waste time arguing about whether it would not be simpler to just go ahead and kill him.

Andres is accustomed to the ignorance of the soldiers because he had encountered it on his other trips through the lines. He is exasperated, however, when the officer displays the same ignorance. All of this, of course, is simply another example of the haphazard way in which the war is being run. If the soldiers were seriously interested in the war, instead of making a dramatic game of it, they would certainly not treat a courier in such a manner. Hemingway shows this ignorance and lack of seriousness most pointedly in the last scene of the chapter. For it is only after Andres has walked behind him for some distance that the officer remembers to take Andres' gun from him.

Chapter 37 shows Jordan's and Maria's last intimate moments together. Jordan feels that he has lived his entire life at this place.

The guerillas are his brothers, his oldest friends; Maria is his wife, his sister, his daughter. Maria, trying to act as a wife would act, tells Jordan that she would like to be by his side in the coming battle. She says, though, that she will help him in any way that he thinks is best.

The scene in the cave at the beginning of Chapter 38 is not a happy one. The men's nerves are taut in anticipation of the fight, and they are making jibing remarks and snapping at each other. Nor is Jordan very happy. The plan which he had concocted during the night does not seem so good now that morning approaches. He snaps angrily at Pilar when she tries to tell him that her palm reading is gypsy nonsense. Then he talks to some of the other men and agrees that he is as nervous as they are.

For the last several chapters, the situation has been growing progressively worse. And this is probably the darkest hour of the book. Jordan does not have enough men to overcome the enemy guard posts, he no longer has the equipment necessary to blow the bridge properly, and he has very little hope that Golz will cancel the attack even if Andres reaches him in time.

The reappearance of Pablo marks what seems to be a turning point in the book. Things immediately begin to look better. With the additional men and horses, the job does not look as impossible as it had seemed. And Pilar, for the first time, shows that Pablo's "going bad" had hurt her deeply. She loves him, and she is proud of him for having come back.

At the beginning of Chapter 39, we discover that Pablo has some pride left also. For he has told the new men that he is still leader of the band, and he asks Jordan not to say anything to "disillusion" them. Pablo's words have a curious effect on Jordan, however. He feels that Pablo's "conversion" is anything but complete. And he is reasonably sure that the man has some other trick up his sleeve.

Chapter 40 begins with the ironic observation that Andres had made his way comparatively rapidly through enemy territory, but had been slowed down once he was behind friendly lines. There, his progress is hampered by ignorance, stupidity, and lack of interest on the part of the soldiers he encounters. Nevertheless, the situation is still looking brighter. In spite of the lack of communication within the Loyalist army and the lack of interest in the war on the part of most of the soldiers — two problems with which the reader is already intimately familiar — Andres continues to make some progress. Finally, he finds two officers who do not fit the mold. They are sympathetic with Andres' problem, and they do everything in their power to aid him in the accomplishment of his mission.

In Chapter 41, everything is "organized confusion" as the pre-battle preparations are made. Jordan's nervousness is shown by his over-zealous repetition of the order that no one is to do anything until sounds of the offensive are heard. Pablo continues to present a problem, but Jordan washes his hands of the whole matter. He will leave on foot after the battle, he says, and the matter of the horses is Pablo's business. He thinks, though, that he is glad he does not know the five new men, whom Pablo will presumably kill for their horses after the battle.

Hemingway's planning is evident to the reader when he sees Jordan and Anselmo return to the spot from which they had earlier observed the bridge. Having already described the terrain, Hemingway does not now have to interrupt the reader's rising excitement with another description. All that he has to do to re-create the picture in the reader's mind is to insert a few reminders of the appearance of the position. At the same time, little by little, the reader is getting a clear idea of the manner in which the coming action will be handled by Jordan and the men.

Jordan temporarily forgets that Anselmo's conscience bothers him about the killing. Anselmo gives him a slight hint, however, and Jordan responds by "ordering" the old man to do what he has been told. Anselmo can thus, at least partially, excuse himself for the killing, since he will be acting under orders.

The next-to-last sentence of the chapter reminds the reader that even the fascists are human beings, living individuals. For Jordan, unable to see the firelight at times, realizes that this is because the man in the sentry box has moved and is standing in front of the brazier.

Irony is packed upon irony in Chapter 42. Despite brief delays, Andres is moving rapidly toward a meeting with Golz, and the reader's hopes continue to rise. When Andres and Gomez encounter another ignorant sentry who seems about to cause them further delay, they are relieved to see Comrade Marty drive up. Marty, a man who should be responsible as well as appreciative of the importance of Andres' mission, is instead a man driven insane by his own importance. He asserts this importance by having Andres and Gomez arrested, thereby causing enough delay so that the two men reach Golz' headquarters too late to see the general himself. Consequently, they have to give the dispatch to Golz' aide, Duval. Though there is, possibly, still enough time to call off the offensive, Duval does not have enough information about the purpose of the attack to make him want to assume the responsibility for canceling it himself. By the time he reaches Golz on the telephone, and discovers that the offensive is not simply a holding attack, it is too late to call it off.

So, here is the crowning irony of the book. Jordan must blow up a bridge, the destruction of which will be absolutely of no value. He must carry out his ineffectual assignment because of the ignorance, stupidity, indifference, and self-importance of people who should most logically have done all they could to help his courier get to his destination in time.

For Whom the Bell Tolls is a tragedy, as are all of Hemingway's novels. However, it is interesting to note in the last chapter how Hemingway's philosophy has developed. At the end of A Farewell to Arms, after Catherine's death, Frederick Henry walks back to his hotel in the rain, helpless and hopeless. At the end of To Have and Have Not, there is at least the implied hope that man will heed Harry Morgan's dying cry, "A man alone ain't got no bloody chance."

The end of For Whom the Bell Tolls shows the reader a more thoughtful and mature Hemingway at his best. The importance of the individual, mentioned in the "Ideology" section of these Notes, is brought out most vividly in Chapter 42. First, Jordan looks through his field glasses at the sentry and sees a human being—a fact which makes him decide not to look at the man again until the fighting begins. Then, Anselmo cries over the killing of the sentry at his end of the bridge. Finally, comes the ultimate irony of the book. Jordan has done everything that he should have done in the way that it ought to have been done, and his mission has been successful. So far as the Cause for which he has been fighting is concerned, his death will serve no useful purpose. Realizing this, Jordan starts to commit suicide as his father had done. But he waits and will die, not for the Cause, but for the protection of an individual, Maria, the symbol of Love.

Notes on Main Characters

The term "major character" must, of course, be a subjective one. Quite often it is not a simple matter to draw a line and say these characters are major and these are minor, and such is the case with *For Whom the Bell Tolls*. Why, the reader might ask, is Maria omitted from the list of major characters? And where is Anselmo? The only answer is that *all* of Hemingway's characters are important, and these two are certainly among the most important of his minor characters. But neither of them can be considered major in relation to their contribution to the central idea represented by Jordan, Pablo, and Pilar. Maria is, simply, the symbol of love and humanity to whom Jordan finds himself becoming attached. She has no political or social feelings of her own; her only interest is in Jordan, not his ideas. And Anselmo, though he does carry an important "thematic load" through the book, is simply the representative of a particular portion of Spanish society, as are most of the other minor characters.

ROBERT JORDAN

Robert Jordan, the protagonist of *For Whom the Bell Tolls*, is a young American college instructor of Spanish who has come to Spain to fight for the Loyalists in the Civil War. He has taken this step, presumably, because of a liberal socio-political philosophy and a broad sympathy for the Spanish people. These feelings closely parallel Hemingway's own attitudes toward the Spanish government and people in the period preceding the war, as described in the "General Introduction" section of these Notes.

By the time the novel opens, however, Jordan has become disenchanted. Since his arrival in Spain, he has come face-to-face with the cynicism of those in power, and his reaction to this cynicism has caused the leaders to laugh at his naivete and to chide him for his "slight political development." Another fact which Jordan has encountered is that most of the common people, regardless of which side they are fighting for, are no longer interested in the war, nor are they very willing to die for the Cause. Having achieved an awareness of these realities, Jordan states clearly in the early pages of the book that he is not a communist, but simply an anti-fascist.

A great deal has been made of the idea that Robert Jordan is not the virile, individualistic hero usually found in Hemingway's writing. To a certain extent, this observation is accurate. Surely the Jordan who existed prior to the opening of the novel, and whom we discover through flashbacks, might have been called a "bleeding-heart liberal" — a highly unusual type of hero for an author of Hemingway's ilk.

The Jordan we see during the actual four-day time span of the novel, however, is a man in transition. Pulled and tugged by ideas of courage and humanity, he moves slowly from a waning belief in the value of the Cause to a new appreciation of the importance of the Individual, and the final impetus to this movement is provided by his love for Maria. In the closing pages of the book, Jordan has done his *duty* for the Cause and lies injured on the hillside, waiting for the communist cavalry. If, at this point, the Cause retained its original importance to him, he would undoubtedly ignore the temptation to commit suicide in order to do more for "the movement" than just his duty. Instead, he does decide to kill himself, but then changes his mind because only by staying alive can he be of service to those *individuals* whose safety is important to him.

And so we have a protagonist who, though not precisely the individualistic hero we might expect from Hemingway, is still a man who has progressed to the conclusion that it is less important to "save the world" than it is to save the individuals in it.

PABLO

Pablo is the leader of the band of guerillas who are supposed to aid Jordan in the demolition of the bridge, the central action of the book. When the reader first encounters Pablo, he finds the man to be sullen and uncooperative, wanting neither himself nor his men to have any part in Jordan's assignment. In a "showdown" with Pilar, his *mujer,* Pablo is forced to abdicate his leadership of the band, and the men decide that they will help Jordan. Pablo's moroseness persists until, on the night before the bridge is to be blown, he runs away. He returns, however, in time to aid in the attack on the bridge.

Hemingway seldom allows a scene, or a piece of action, or a bit of dialog to carry only a single meaning. In the same way, he seldom permits his major ideas to be represented by a single character. Though, at first, Pablo and Jordan seem to be greatly dissimilar, as the book progresses, the reader becomes increasingly aware that the two men are basically alike. Both men are experiencing the same sort of transition, the major difference being that Pablo has progressed farther along the scale than Jordan. He has already accepted those realities of the war to which Jordan has been trying to adapt himself, and he has already lost that fervor which he had at the beginning of "the movement." In addition, Pablo is less willing than Jordan to deceive himself about the possibility of doing the bridge assignment successfully.

Sick of the war and unwilling to die for the *cause,* Pablo deserts, an action which is thematically parallel to Jordan's later contemplation of suicide. But, again paralleling Jordan's action, he returns because he is the only one who can lead the group to safety after the battle. "Having done such a thing [i.e., deserted]," he says, "there is a loneliness that cannot be borne."

PILAR

Pilar is the gypsy *mujer* of Pablo. She has been with him for several years, and one of the purposes she serves in the book is to give the reader background information. It is through her that we see the beginning of "the movement," the way life was before the war, and the courage of Pablo before he "went bad." Pilar also plays a major part, through references to her reading of Jordan's palm, in maintaining the feeling of impending doom.

But even these purposes are not enough for Hemingway. As mentioned above in relation to Pablo, Hemingway does not let his major idea be represented by one character alone. In the book we see Robert Jordan in transition from one concept to another. Pablo, too, is on that same road, a few miles, as it were, ahead of Jordan. And now we find Pilar traveling the same road, but "bringing up the rear." It is she who supplies the allegiance to the *cause* which is dead in Pablo and dying in Jordan. "I am for the Republic," she says, in her showdown with Pablo, "and the Republic is the bridge." She is late, too, in her realization of the real danger involved in the bridge assignment. And it is only in the final pages of the book that she reaches that stage of her transition in which she begins to doubt the value of the *cause*.

One of the major ideas of the book, then, is the transition, from one belief to another, of the three characters described above. By placing each of these characters at a different stage of development, Hemingway has enabled himself to portray the three stages of this transition and yet retain the emotional intensity provided by the brief time span covered by the book.

The Hemingway Code Hero*

Indigenous to almost all of Hemingway's novels and in fact to a study of Hemingway in general is the concept of the Hemingway hero, sometimes more popularly known as the "code hero." When Hemingway's novels first began to appear they were readily accepted by the American reading public; in fact, they were enthusiastically received. Part of this reception was due to the fact that Hemingway had created a new type of fictional character whose basic response to life appealed very strongly to the people of the 1920's. At first the average reader saw in the Hemingway hero a type of person whom he could identify with in almost a dream sense. The Hemingway man was a man's man. He was a man involved in a great deal of drinking. He was a man who moved from one love affair to another, who participated in wild game hunting, who enjoyed bullfights, who was involved in all of the so-called manly activities which the typical American male did not participate in.

As more and more of Hemingway's novels appeared and the reader became more familiar with this type of person, we gradually began to formulate a theory about the Hemingway code hero. We observed that throughout many of Hemingway's novels the code hero acts in a manner which allowed the critic to formulate a particular code. It must be emphasized, however, that the Hemingway character or code hero would himself never speak of a code. He does not make such broad generalizations. To actually formulate a set of rules of conduct to which the Hemingway character would adhere is, in one sense, a violation of the essential nature of the code hero. He does not talk about what he believes in. He is a man of action rather than a man of theory. Therefore, the following concepts of the code hero are those enunciated not by the hero himself but by the critics and readers who are familiar with the total body of Hemingway's works and of his views.

Behind the formulation of this concept of the hero lies the basic disillusionment of the American public, the disillusionment that was

*"The Hemingway Code Hero," by James L. Roberts, reprinted from *A Farewell to Arms Notes*, copyright 1966 by Cliff's Notes, Inc.

brought about by the First World War. The sensitive man in America or the sensitive man in the world came to the realization that the old concepts and old values embedded in Christianity and other ethical systems of the western world had not served to save mankind from the catastrophe of this World War. Consequently, after the war many sensitive writers began to look for a new system of values, a system of values that would replace the old received doctrines that had proved to be useless. Having endured the great calamity of World War I, Hemingway found that he could not return to the quiet countryside of America, could no longer accept those values that had previously dominated all of America. Instead, he searched for some principles based upon a sense of order and discipline that would endure in any particular situation. We can conclude this by saying that Hemingway's values then are not Christian, they are not the morals that we have grown accustomed to in twentieth-century Protestant America.

A basis for all of the actions of all Hemingway key heroes is the concept of death. The idea of death permeates or lies behind all of the characters' actions in Hemingway's novels. This view involves Hemingway's concept that "when you are dead you are dead." There is nothing more. If man cannot accept a life or reward after death, the emphasis must then be on obtaining or doing or perform-ing something in this particular life. If death ends all activity, if death ends all knowledge and consciousness, man must seek his reward here, now, immediately. Consequently, the Hemingway man exists in a large part for the gratification of his sensual desires, he will devote himself to all types of physical pleasures because these are the rewards of this life.

Hemingway's characters first attracted attention because they did drink a lot and did have many love affairs. This appealed on a simple level to the populace. In its most elementary sense, if man is to face total oblivion at his death, there is nothing then to do but enjoy as many of the physical pleasures as possible during this life. Thus the Hemingway man will drink, he will make love, he will enjoy food, he will enjoy all sensuous appetites—all the sensuous pleasures that are possible. For example, we need only to recall small insignifi-cant scenes in Hemingway works, such as in *A Farewell to Arms*,

when in the midst of the battle Frederick Henry and his two ambulance drivers sit down in the middle of the battlefield amid all of the
destruction and thoroughly devote themselves to relishing, enjoying,
savoring every taste of their macaroni, cheese, and bottle of mediocre wine.

Returning to the primary consideration, that is, that death is the
end of all things, it then becomes the duty and the obligation of the
Hemingway hero to avoid death at almost all cost. Life must continue. Life is valuable and enjoyable. Life is everything. Death is
nothing. With this view in mind it might seem strange then to the
casual or superficial reader that the Hemingway code hero will often
be placed in an encounter with death, or that the Hemingway hero
will choose often to confront death. The bullfighters, the wild game
hunters, characters like these are in constant confrontation with
death. From this we derive then the idea of *grace under pressure*.
This concept is one according to which the character must act in a
way that is acceptable when he is faced with the fact of death. One
might express it in other terms by saying that the Hemingway man
must have fear of death, but he must not be afraid to die. By fear
we mean that he must have the intellectual realization that death
is the end of all things and as such must constantly be avoided in
one way or another.

But—and this is the significant point—man can never act in a
cowardly way. He must not show that he is afraid or trembling or
frightened in the presence of death. We can extend this idea further
by saying that, if man wishes to live, he lives most intensely sometimes when he is in the direct presence of death. This will at times
bring out man's most innate qualities, test his manhood, will con-
tribute then an intensity, a vivacity to the life that he is at present
leading, and it is for this reason that Hemingway often places his
characters either in war, in bullfighting rings, or on the plains of
Africa where he must face an animal determined to kill him. It is
then that the Hemingway man shows the coolness, the grace, the
courage, the discipline which have prompted the idea of grace under
pressure. The man who never encounters death, who never faces
any danger at all, this man has not yet been tested; we don't know
whether he will withstand the pressures, whether he will prove to
be a true Hemingway man.

Thus in the short story "The Short, Happy Life of Francis Macomber," at the age of thirty-five Francis himself had never tested his courage. On the first test he ran; he ran like a coward. But on a subsequent test he stood up and proved himself to be a true, good Hemingway hero. It is thus only by testing, by coming into confrontation with something that is dangerous that man lives with this intensity. In the presence of death, then, man can discover his own sense of being, his own potentiality.

THE *NADA* CONCEPT

Aside from death being a part of the concept of the code hero, there are certain images that are often connected with this view. His actions are often identified by certain definite movements or performances. He is often called a restless man. By restless is meant that he will often stay awake at nighttime and sleep all during the day. The reason for this is that for the Hemingway man sleep itself is a type of obliteration of the consciousness. Night is a difficult time for the Hemingway hero or code hero because night itself — the darkness of night — implies, suggests, or symbolizes the utter darkness that man will have to face after death. Therefore the code hero will avoid nighttime. This will be the time he will drink; this will be the time he will carouse or stay awake. In many novels he will spend the night making love with someone and only at the crack of dawn will he then desire sleep.

In *A Farewell to Arms*, Frederick Henry stays awake all night so as to be with Catherine Barkley, who is on the night shift. Catherine Barkley is on the night shift so that they will not have to sleep during the night; they can make love during the night, or talk. They can do anything to avoid the combination of darkness and sleep. In short stories such as "The Clean, Well-Lighted Place" the emphasis is upon light. The Hemingway code character, if he goes to sleep at night, will often leave a light on. He does not like the darkness of the room, the darkness of the night, the state of sleeping, because these are in themselves suggestive of that final sleep of death.

THE DISCIPLINE OF THE CODE HERO

If the old traditional values are no good anymore, if they will not serve man, what values then will serve man? Hemingway rejects things of abstract qualities—courage, loyalty, honesty, bravery. These are all just words. What Hemingway would prefer to have are concrete things. For Hemingway a man can be courageous in battle on Tuesday morning at 10 o'clock. But this does not mean that he will be courageous on Wednesday morning at 9 o'clock. A single act of courage does not mean that a man is by nature courageous. Or a man who has been courageous in war might not be courageous in some civil affair or in some other human endeavor. What Hemingway is searching for are absolute values, which will be the same, which will be constant at every moment of every day and of every day of every week.

Courage itself, then, is a relative value. It might be true for one moment but not true for the next. As he expressed it in his novel *A Farewell to Arms:* "I was always embarrassed by the words sacred, glorious, and sacrifice and the expression in vain. . . . Abstract words such as glory, honor, courage, or hallow were obscene beside the concrete names of villages, the numbers of roads, the names of rivers, the numbers of regiments and the dates." The quotation indicates then that Hemingway is searching for concrete things that one can feel, touch, and see. The name of a place is something that a man knows.

Ultimately therefore, for Hemingway the only value that will serve man is an innate faculty of self-discipline. This is a value that grows out of man's essential being, in his inner nature. If a man has discipline to face one thing on one day he will still possess that same degree of discipline on another day and in another situation. Thus Francis Macomber in the short story "The Short, Happy Life of Francis Macomber," has faced a charging animal, and once he has had the resolution to stand and confront this charging beast, he has developed within himself a discipline that will serve him in all situations. This control can function in almost any way in a Hemingway work.

We have said earlier that the Hemingway man drinks a lot and yet the Hemingway man is never a sloppy drunk. Such people as Mike Campbell in *The Sun Also Rises* often prove to be non-Hemingway characters. The sloppy drunk is rejected. The man who cannot hold his liquor does not possess the proper degree of discipline. It is fine to drink, to drink an immense amount. But to get to the point that a man does not know what he is doing, denotes lack of the discipline that is necessary to a code hero. If a man does not know what he is doing from having drunk too much, he is no longer in possession of his own faculties. Thus a typical Hemingway character is a man who is always in control of the situation, who has the discipline to handle any particular given circumstance.

This discipline functions in other ways also. For example, the Hemingway hero will often say, "don't let's not talk about it." This means after he has performed some act of bravery he will not discuss it. Talking is emotionalism. It is the action that is important. If you talk about the act too much you lose the importance of the act itself. Even after two characters have made love they do not talk about it. This is a type of discipline also, the discipline of refusing to be emotional about an event. If a character ever expresses any emotion he is often ashamed of having done so. You lose the value of any act by talking too much about it.

The Hemingway code hero is also a person of some degree of skill. It is seldom mentioned what the character does, but we do know that Robert Jordan in *For Whom the Bell Tolls* is an excellent teacher of Spanish. We also know that Frederick Henry has been a good architect and that Jake Barnes is a highly competent journalist. In *A Farewell to Arms* Rinaldi devotes himself completely to his surgical operations. It is in the act of doing that which a man is good at doing that the code character finds himself. Rinaldi makes the statement that he only lives while he is performing an operation. Thus the Hemingway hero will be a person who possesses some skill and who is highly competent at that particular skill. On the contrary, he detests people who are mediocre. There are enough people who are like the Hemingway hero that he will not associate with the ordinary or mediocre person. The Hemingway hero feels that if he is not accepted in one group he makes no intentions to join that group.

In *The Sun Also Rises* Jake Barnes cannot understand why people like Robert Cohn keep hanging around where they are not wanted. Jake Barnes knows that there are enough people in the world who think like him, who like him, so that he has no intention of associating with people of another nature.

This attitude leads to the concept of the loyalty that a Hemingway hero feels for other people. He feels an intense loyalty for a small group of people. In *A Farewell to Arms* we find that Frederick Henry deserts the Italian army because the Italian army is abstract. The concept of the national government is also abstract. However, the loyalty that he feels to his small individual group, that is, the group of ambulance drivers, is very important. This concept is later modified in *For Whom the Bell Tolls* because Robert Jordan does feel a sense of loyalty to the Spanish land. He enters the war partly for this reason. But his most intense feelings of loyalty are for a small guerilla band with whom he works behind the lines in Spain. Again a sense of loyalty is expressed in *The Old Man and the Sea* between the young boy and the fisherman. In any case, the Hemingway hero cannot feel a sense of loyalty to something abstract, but as far as the intense personal immediate friendship is concerned, he is totally devoted to this smaller, this more personal, group.

In conclusion, the Hemingway hero is a man whose concepts are shaped by his view of death, that in the face of death a man must perform certain acts and these acts often involve enjoying or taking the most he can from life. The Hemingway man will not talk about his concepts. Thus to formulate them as we have done here is a violation of the concept. He is a man of intense loyalty to a small group because he cannot accept things abstract. He must need the definite, the concrete. He does not talk too much. He expresses himself not in words but in actions. Consequently, most of Hemingway's novels are based upon action. The Hemingway hero then is not a thinker; he is a man of action. But his acts are based upon a concept of life.

Ideology

"No man is an *Iland*, intire of it selfe; every man is a peece of the *Continent*, a part of the maine; if a *Clod* bee washed away by the *Sea*, *Europe* is the lesse, as well as if a *Promontorie* were, as well as if a *Mannor* of thy *friends* or of *thine owne* were, any mans *death* diminishes *me*, because I am involved in *Mankinde*; And therefore never send to know for whom the *bell* tolls; It tolls for *thee*."

The above quotation from John Donne appears facing the first page of the text of *For Whom the Bell Tolls*. It is a dramatic, concise statement of the major theme of the novel—the dual importance of man as an individual and as an integral part of "Mankinde."

The question of the importance of the individual is, of course, one of the more serious points in the argument between the liberal and conservative philosophies. And it is a question with which Hemingway has dealt before. Many of the heroes of his early stories and novels were go-it-alone individualists, and he had been claimed by the conservatives as their spokesman. But when, at the end of *To Have and Have Not*, the dying protagonist, Harry Morgan, said, "A man alone ain't got no bloody chance," the liberals rejoiced. They claimed that a new period of social consciousness had developed in Hemingway's writing, and they quickly adopted him as the spokesman for their cause.

When *For Whom the Bell Tolls* appeared, liberals and conservatives alike declared that Hemingway had deserted them. In the early pages of the book, the hero, Robert Jordan, states unequivocally that he is not a communist, but simply an anti-fascist. As the novel develops, so does Jordan's realization of man's dual importance as individual as well as social being, and it is because of this realization that he insists on being left to die at the end of the book.

For Whom the Bell Tolls is, as are all great novels, somewhat like a symphony in that it has a number of themes which appear, disappear, and then reappear as the story progresses. The major, overall theme of irony, the theme of mysticism, and the love theme — are treated in the commentaries at the end of the appropriate chapters.

Style

From almost the beginning of his writing career, Hemingway's distinctive style occasioned a great deal of comment and controversy. Basically, his style is simple, direct, and unadorned, probably as a result of his early newspaper training. He avoids the adjective whenever possible, but because he is a master at transmitting emotion without the flowery prose of his Victorian novelist predecessors, the effect is far more telling. In *Observations on the Style of Ernest Hemingway,* from "Contexts of Criticism" by Harry Levin (Harvard University Press, 1957), the critic says:

> Hemingway puts his emphasis on nouns because, among other parts of speech, they come closest to things. Stringing them along by means of conjunctions, he approximates the actual flow of experience.

Hemingway has often been described as a master of dialog, and most readers agree, upon being first introduced to his writing, that "this is the way these characters would *really* talk." It is interesting to note, however, that Hemingway's one attempt at playwriting was a failure. Actually, a close examination of his dialog will reveal that this is rarely the way people really speak. The effect is accomplished, rather, by the calculated emphasis and repetition which makes us remember what has been said.

Since the critics cannot entirely agree on Hemingway's style, perhaps the best way is to put it into the author's own words. Shortly before his tragic death, Hemingway gave to the Wisdom Foundation in California a collection of his observations on life and art, love and death. They were published in the January, 1963, issue of *Playboy* magazine, and in them Hemingway said of his writing:

> I do most of my work in my head. I never begin to write until my ideas are in order. Frequently I recite passages of dialogue as it is being written; the ear is a good censor. I never set down a sentence on paper until I have it so expressed that it will be clear to anyone.

Yet, I sometimes think that my style is suggestive rather than direct. The reader must often use his imagination or lose the most subtle part of my thoughts.

I take great pains with my work, pruning and revising with a tireless hand. I have the welfare of my creations very much at heart. I cut them with infinite care, and burnish them until they become brilliants. What many another writer would be content to leave in massive proportions, I polish into a tiny gem.

Hemingway goes on at some length, but the essence of what he says may be in this paragraph:

A writer's style should be direct and personal, his imagery rich and earthy, and his words simple and vigorous. The greatest writers have the gift of brilliant brevity, are hard workers, diligent scholars and competent stylists.

To explain Hemingway's style adequately in a few paragraphs is impossible. Scores of articles, and even some books, have been written on the subject, and it is to these that the serious student should go for additional, more detailed information.

Review Questions and
Theme Topics

1. How does Hemingway go about giving the reader information about his characters?

2. How does Hemingway give the members of the guerilla band distinct personalities?

3. Pablo has "gone bad." What does that mean? How is it shown? How does it affect Jordan?

4. How is Jordan's feeling for Maria shown? What makes the reader feel that it is really love?

5. How do Jordan's feelings about his father and grandfather affect him?

6. How are chapter lengths used to give emotional tone?

7. Why does Hemingway skip back and forth between Jordan and Andres in the last part of the book?

8. What is the effect on the reader of the delays encountered by Andres? What aspects of the war are brought out by this device?

9. Discuss several examples of Hemingway's theme of irony in the book.

10. Discuss the religious theme of the book as it is shown in Jordan. Anselmo? Joaquin?

11. Why did Hemingway include Pilar's tale of the atrocities committed by the Loyalists?

12. Discuss the development of Pilar's character. Of Pablo's.

13. How do the Spanish feel about the intervention of foreigners in their civil war?

14. Why is Kashkin mentioned so often? Why does Pilar bring up the subject of Kashkin in the scene at El Sordo's camp?

15. How does Hemingway weave premonitions of tragedy into the book? How do they affect the reader? Jordan?

16. How does Hemingway give the reader the feeling that the dialog is in Spanish? Would it make any difference in the effect of the book if this device had not been used? Why?

17. Discuss the characters in the book whose primary purpose seems to be to offer comic relief.

18. How does El Sordo treat Jordan in the book? What is the significance of this treatment? What does the reader know about El Sordo before his death?

19. Why does Hemingway make the fascists in the book human beings? How does he go about doing this?

20. Have Jordan's political convictions changed since the beginning of the war? Do they change in the period covered by the book? How? Why?

21. Why is Pilar's story of the bullfighter included in the book?

22. Discuss several reasons for Jordan's having come to Spain to fight in the civil war.

23. How are the airplanes used to deepen the emotional effect of the book?

24. How does Hemingway go about giving the reader information as to what sort of life the peasants led before the revolution.

54

25. Discuss two or more scenes in the book which show the importance of the individual. Discuss two or more scenes which show the importance of the Cause for which the Loyalists are fighting.

Selected Bibliography

Baker, Carlos. *Hemingway: The Writer as Artist,* 2nd ed. Princeton: Princeton University Press, 1956.

——(ed.). *Hemingway and His Critics: An International Anthology.* New York: Hill & Wang, 1961.

——(ed.). *Ernest Hemingway: Critiques of Four Major Novels,* A Scribner Research Anthology. New York: Charles Scribner's Sons, 1962.

Fenton, Charles A. *The Apprenticeship of Ernest Hemingway: The Early Years.* New York: Farrar, Straus & Cudahy, 1954.

Hemingway, Leicester. *My Brother, Ernest Hemingway.* Cleveland: World Publishing Co., 1962.

Hotchner, A. E. *Papa Hemingway: A Personal Memoir.* New York: Random House, 1966.

McCaffery, John K. M. (ed.). *Ernest Hemingway, The Man and His Work.* Cleveland: World Publishing Co., 1950.

Weeks, Robert P. (ed.). *Hemingway: A Collection of Critical Essays.* Englewood Cliffs, N.J.: Prentice-Hall, 1962.

Young, Philip. *Ernest Hemingway.* New York: Rinehart & Co., 1952.

——. *Ernest Hemingway,* University of Minnesota Pamphlets on American Writers, No. 1. Minneapolis: University of Minnesota Press, 1959.

NOTES